Should Citizens Be Required to

VOTE?

By Leslie Beckett

Published in 2019 by
KidHaven Publishing, an Imprint of Greenhaven Publishing, LLC
353 3rd Avenue
Suite 255
New York, NY 10010

Designer: Deanna Paternostro
Editor: Katie Kawa

Photo credits: Cover Blend Images - Hill Street Studios/Brand X Pictures/Getty Images; p. 5 (top) Robin Lynne Gibson/Photolibrary/Getty Images; p. 5 (bottom) fstop123/E+/Getty Images; p. 7 Asanka Brendon Ratnayake/Lonely Planet Images/Getty Images; p. 9 YURI CORTEZ/AFP/Getty Images; p. 11 J.michael.watkins/Wikimedia Commons; p. 13 Joseph Sohm/Shutterstock.com; p. 15 sirtravelalot/Shutterstock.com; p. 17 Rawpixel.com/Shutterstock.com; p. 19 MARK RALSTON/AFP/Getty Images; p. 21 (notepad) ESB Professional/Shutterstock.com; p. 21 (markers) Kucher Serhii/Shutterstock.com; p. 21 (photo frame) FARBAI/iStock/Thinkstock; p. 21 (inset, left) Gino Santa Maria/Shutterstock.com; p. 21 (inset, middle-left) Everett Historical/Shutterstock.com; p. 21 (inset, middle-right) Rob Crandall/Shutterstock.com; p. 21 (inset, right) Jason Kolenda/Shutterstock.com.

Cataloging-in-Publication Data

Names: Beckett, Leslie.
Title: Should citizens be required to vote? / Leslie Beckett.
Description: New York : KidHaven Publishing, 2019. | Series: Points of view | Includes glossary and index.
Identifiers: ISBN 9781534527690 (pbk.) | ISBN 9781534527713 (library bound) | ISBN 9781534527706 (6 pack) | ISBN 9781534527720 (ebook)
Subjects: LCSH: Voting–United States–Juvenile literature. | Elections–United States–Juvenile literature. | Political participation–United States–Juvenile literature. | Democracy–United States–Juvenile literature.
Classification: LCC JK1978.B435 2019 | DDC 323.60973–dc23
Printed in the United States of America

CPSIA compliance information: Batch #BW19KL: For further information contact Greenhaven Publishing LLC, New York, New York at 1-844-317-7404.

Please visit our website, www.greenhavenpublishing.com. For a free color catalog of all our high-quality books, call toll free 1-844-317-7404 or fax 1-844-317-7405.

CONTENTS

Different Views on
VOTING

The United States is a democracy. This means its citizens have a say in how their country is run. They vote to choose their leaders and to make their voices heard on important issues.

Some countries believe voting is so important that their citizens are required to vote and are **punished** if they don't. This isn't the case in the United States, but some people believe it should be. Others, however, think people should be free to choose to vote or not to vote. These different points of view play a part in how democracies work around the world.

Know the Facts!

According to a 2017 study, 91 percent of Americans believe having the right to vote is an important part of feeling free.

Some people think making voting mandatory, or required, would make American democracy stronger. Other people feel it would take away certain freedoms that are valued by Americans. Learning about both sides of this **debate** will help you make your own informed, or educated, opinion.

How Does Compulsory
VOTING WORK?

When voting is mandatory in a country, it's called a compulsory voting system. It works differently in different countries. Generally, it means that all people over a certain age are required to register, or sign up, to vote. These people are also required to vote in elections.

In most cases, if people don't vote, they have to pay a small fine. If a person has a good reason for not being able to vote, such as being sick, they don't have to pay the fine. In some countries, people over a certain age also aren't punished if they don't vote.

Know the Facts!

More than 700 million people around the world live in countries that require their citizens to vote.

One country that has compulsory voting is Australia. If an adult in Australia doesn't vote at a polling center, such as the one shown here, and doesn't have a good reason for not voting, they have to pay a fine of around $20.

People who support compulsory voting often point to the other countries around the world that have made voting mandatory. They believe these countries are examples of how compulsory voting can make people more active citizens.

More than 20 countries around the world require their citizens to vote. The number of people who vote in those countries has generally stayed the same over the last 70 years. However, in countries that don't have compulsory voting, the amount of people who vote has dropped by as much as 10 percent over the same period of time.

Know the Facts!

Between 1945 and 2015, around 85 percent of people in countries that made voting mandatory actually voted.

Citizens are required to vote in many Latin American countries, such as Mexico, shown here. Many people believe making voting mandatory in these countries has **encouraged** more people to take an active part in shaping their government.

A Loss of LIBERTY

People who oppose having a compulsory voting system in the United States believe it might be good for other countries but it goes against American values. They see the United States as a country that was founded on the idea that people should be free to act without a government telling them what to do. Compulsory voting is a way for the government to tell people they have to vote.

Many Americans don't like when the government forces them to do something. They believe it goes against their rights and takes away important freedoms, or liberties.

Know the Facts!

A 2017 study showed that 20 percent of Americans believe voting should be mandatory, while 78 percent believe it should be a choice left up to each person.

The Declaration of Independence was written in 1776. It stated that Americans didn't want to be controlled by the British government. Since then, American citizens have often disliked the idea of the government trying to control their actions, such as voting.

Turning Around Low Voter
TURNOUT

In the United States, people are free to choose not to vote. As time has gone on, more and more Americans have started making that choice. In the 2016 U.S. presidential election, only about 55 percent of the Americans who could vote actually voted.

Supporters of compulsory voting believe making voting mandatory would increase voter turnout by bringing more people into the democratic **process**. It would also encourage people to become more informed about their government because they have to take a more active part in it.

Know the Facts!

A group called the Organisation for Economic Co-operation and Development (OECD) has tracked voting in **developed** democracies around the world. On its list of countries ranked by voter turnout, the United States was 28th out of 35.

Voter turnout measures the people who are registered to vote who actually vote on Election Day. The United States has had very low voter turnout in recent years, and people are looking for ways to fix this, such as making voting mandatory.

More Voters, More
PROBLEMS

Compulsory voting systems require citizens to vote. However, they don't require citizens to vote in an informed way. Some citizens might choose to learn more about the candidates, or people running for office, if they have to vote for them, but many don't choose to do this.

In countries where voting is mandatory, some people fill out their **ballots** with the names of people who aren't actually running for office. Others turn in a blank ballot or don't fill out the whole ballot. This shows that compulsory voting might improve voter turnout, but it doesn't always make people more active and informed citizens.

Know the Facts!

In Australia, people sometimes cast what are known as donkey votes. These people pick the candidates in the order they're listed in on the ballot because they're forced to vote.

Requiring people to vote leads to a higher number of votes cast but not always a higher quality. Many people still choose to do other things instead of learning about what they're voting for, so they turn in blank ballots or vote without any real thought.

HEARD

In a compulsory voting system, even if voters aren't always informed, they're still making their voices heard. Many people believe those voices can help a country better serve all its citizens.

Certain groups of people are more likely to vote than others. For example, the United States has two main **political parties**: Democrats and Republicans. More Republicans than Democrats chose to vote in the 2016 presidential election. White Americans also had better voter turnout than people of other races. Compulsory voting would cause people from groups who vote in smaller numbers to become a bigger part of the democratic process.

Know the Facts!

Since 1996, the number of Latinx people—whose families come from Latin America—who could vote in a U.S. election but chose not to has been larger than the number of Latinx people who actually voted.

People who support compulsory voting believe it can create a government that better **represents** all its citizens because all citizens have to vote.

Not Fixing the
PROBLEM

If citizens were required to vote, it would help **solve** the problem of low voter turnout. However, it would do this by forcing people to vote rather than dealing with the reasons why they choose not to vote.

People choose not to vote for many reasons. Some feel their vote doesn't matter, while others don't trust the government. In many cases, people choose not to vote as a way to show they don't like any of the people running for office. Forcing them to vote doesn't fix those problems.

Know the Facts!

During the 2016 U.S. presidential election, 25 percent of the people who chose not to vote made that choice because they didn't like the people running or the things they stood for.

Many people chose not to vote in the 2016 U.S. presidential election because they didn't like Donald Trump or Hillary Clinton—the two main candidates. They believed that not voting was a way to show their **disappointment** with the people running.

A Choice or a
DUTY?

People have made many other arguments in favor of and against compulsory voting. Some believe it would let candidates spend more time talking about issues and less time trying to get people to vote. Others believe it could never work because it would be too hard to **enforce**.

Voting is often seen as one of the most important things a citizen can do in a democracy. Do you think it's a right people should be able to choose to exercise or a duty they should be forced to do?

Know the Facts!

In the United States, a person must be at least 18 years old to vote.

Should citizens be required to vote?

YES

- Other countries around the world have compulsory voting.

- Compulsory voting forces people to become more active citizens and raises voter turnout rates.

- When all citizens have to vote, the voices of all citizens are heard.

- Candidates can spend more time talking about issues and less time telling people to vote.

NO

- Requiring people to vote takes away their freedom.

- More votes are cast, but they're often not informed votes.

- Forcing people to vote doesn't fix the problems that have led people to choose not to vote.

- It costs money and can often be hard to enforce compulsory voting.

A chart such as this one is often a helpful tool for understanding different points of view and forming your own opinion.

GLOSSARY

ballot: A sheet of paper used to cast a secret vote.

debate: An argument or discussion about an issue, generally between two sides.

developed: Advanced.

disappointment: Unhappiness caused by someone or something that fails to meet hopes or expectations.

encourage: To make a person more likely to do something.

enforce: To make sure people do what is required by a rule or law.

political party: A group whose members hold the same general beliefs about how government should work.

process: A set of actions.

punish: To make someone suffer for doing something wrong.

represent: To act officially or stand for someone or something.

solve: To fix or find the answer to a problem.

For More
INFORMATION

WEBSITES

Kids Voting USA

www.kidsvotingusa.org/

The Kids Voting program teaches young people about the democratic process, and its website has information about how kids can participate as well as fun activities.

PBS Kids: You Choose

pbskids.org/youchoose

This website has videos, activities, and facts about voting and the people Americans vote for.

BOOKS

Almasy, Kip. *Why Voting Matters.* New York, NY: PowerKids Press, 2018.

Boothroyd, Jennifer. *What Are Elections?* Minneapolis, MN: Lerner Publishing Group, 2016.

Spilsbury, Louise, and Mike Gordon. *Vote for Me!: How Governments and Elections Work Around the World.* Hauppauge, NY: Barron's Educational Series, 2018.

INDEX